INDIAN RECIPES

VEGETARIAN

The Publisher would like to thank
Hotel Holiday Inn Crown Plaza, New Delhi and
Maurya Sheraton Hotel and Towers, New Delhi
for the preparation of the dishes, and for giving
permission to photograph them.

ISBN: 1-85605-294-X

Published by **Blitz Editions**
an imprint of
Bookmart Limited
Registered Number 2372865
Trading as Bookmart Limited
Desford Road
Enderby, Leicester, LE9 5AD

Project Coordinator: Padmini Mehta
Photographs: Neeraj Paul & Dheeraj Paul
Design: Sarita Verma Mathur
Typesetting: Monika Gupta

Printed and bound by
Star Standard Industries Pte. Ltd., Singapore

INDIAN RECIPES
*
VEGETARIAN

Blitz Editions

INTRODUCTION

Eating vegetarian is the healthier way to be, as many people are beginning to discover. It is time to bring about a diet transformation and what better way than through the palate-tingling exotic Indian vegetarian cuisine.

India has for centuries had the largest number of vegetarians in the world and consequently has developed an extremely versatile vegetarian cuisine. It is easy to be a vegetarian in a country with such a wealth and variety of vegetables. It is possible to eat a different meal each day of the year and still have recipes to spare. The vegetables change with the seasons giving the palate a kaleidoscope adventure.

Vegetables taste best when cooked with a minimum of fat and spices on medium heat to bring out the most unusual and delicious natural flavours. Vegetables are usually lightly spiced, stir fried and left to cook until tender. Or they could be curried in a puree of onions and tomatoes, garlic and ginger. But there are thousands of regional variations.

Vegetables are supplemented with dals and paneer, salads and raitas, pickles and chutneys to make a wholesome meal and an attractive presentation at the table.

The majority of recipes are simple and health conscious . The book includes recipes from traditional kitchens, which have been simplified keeping in mind your needs.

VEGETARIAN

❊

Stuffed Potatoes	6
Potatoes in Spinach Sauce	8
Potato Saagu	10
Potato & Sago Pattie	11
Gobi Gulistan	12
Guncha-o-Keema	14
Kadhai Paneer	16
Dum Saunfia Tikka	18
Paneer Do Piaza	19
Pickled Cottage Cheese	20
Paneer Dahi ke Kebab	22
Kalyani Paneer Tikka	24
Paneer Capsicum Delite	25
Mushrooms with Peas and Spring Onons	26
Curried Spinach Balls	28
Hara Kebab	30
Kadhai Mushroom	31
Masala Dosa	32
Idli	34
Dal Vadas	36
Rasam	37
Sambhar	38
Hyderabadi Mirchi ka Salan	40
Fried Okra	42
Chana Pindi	44
Dal Amritsari	45
Spiced Sambhar with Rice	46
Khud Pukht Qureshi	48
Tamatar ka Shorba	49
Raseele Kum-Kum	50
Besan ke Gatte	52
Karele Masale Wale	54
Anokhi Biryani	56
Morrels Pulao	57
Tandoori Salad	58
Mint Relish	59
Mixed Raita	60
Spiced Yoghurt	61

STUFFED POTATOES

SERVES: 4

Locally known as *Dum Alu Bhojpuri.*

— *Ingredients* —

Potatoes, small round (20-25 pcs) — *600 gms*

Potatoes (boiled and grated) — *200 gms*

For the gravy:

Bay leaf (tej patta) — *1*

Black cumin seeds (shah jeera) — *3 gms/²/₃ tsp*

Cloves — *6*

Cinnamon sticks — *2*

Garam masala — *10 gms/2* tsp or

Garlic paste — *30 gms/2 tbs*

Ghee (clarified butter) — *15 gms/1 tbs*

Ginger paste — *30 gms/2 tbs*

Green cardamoms — *6*

Lemon juice — *15 ml/1 tbs*

Onions, grated — *80 gms/5¹/₃ tbs*

Red chilli powder — *10 gms/2 tsp*

Refined oil — *50 ml/3¹/₃ tbs*

Turmeric powder (haldi) — *5 gms/1 tsp*

Yoghurt, whisked — *150 gms/ ¾ cup*

Salt to taste

— *Steps* —

1. Heat the ghee in a pan. Add half the grated onions, ginger and garlic pastes and fry for 4-5 minutes. Add boiled and grated potatoes, half the red chilli powder, turmeric powder and garam masala. Season with lemon juice and salt. Keep aside.

2. Boil and peel the small potatoes. Scoop and hollow them.

3. Fry these potatoes carefully and stuff each potato with the potato mixture of Step 1. Keep aside covered.

4. Heat the refined oil in a pan over medium heat. Add bay leaf, cinnamon sticks, cloves, green cardamoms, black cumin seed and fry for 30-50 seconds or until they begin to crackle.

5. Add the remaining grated onions, ginger and garlic pastes and fry for 2-3 minutes.

6. Add turmeric powder and red chilli powder and fry over medium heat for 5-6 minutes.

7. Add whisked yoghurt. Stir and cook till moisture evaporates. Add remaining garam masala. Season to taste with salt.

8. Arrange the stuffed potatoes carefully inside the pan. Sprinkle lemon juice.

9. Cover the lid. Cook for 3-4 minutes on very low heat.

TIPS

Time: Preparation: 20 minutes
Cooking: 20 minutes

To serve: Transfer to a serving platter and garnish with chopped coriander, ginger juliennes and lace with fresh cream. Serve with rice/pooris.

POTATOES IN SPINACH SAUCE

SERVES: 4

Exotically named *Zanat-e-Numa.*

— Ingredients —

Potatoes — *1 kg*
Spinach — *400 gms*
Clarified butter (*ghee*)
— *30 ml/2 tbs*
Cooking oil for gravy
— *90 ml/6 tbs*
Cooking oil to deep fry
Coriander leaves
— *90 gms/6 tbs*
Coriander powder
— *5 gms/1 tsp*
Cumin (*jeera*) seeds
— *2.5 gms/½ tsp*
Dry mango powder
(*amchur*) — *5 gms/1 tsp*
Fenugreek (*methi*), fresh
— *105 gms/7 tbs*
Garam masala — *5 gms/1 tsp*
Green chillies — *10*
Mint — *45 gms/3 tbs*
Raisins — *20 gms/4 tsp*
Red chilli powder
— *10 gms/2 tsp*
Tomatoes, chopped
— *80 gms/⅓ cup*

Turmeric (*haldi*) powder
— *2.5 gms/½ tsp*
Yoghurt — *45 gms/3 tbs*
Salt to taste

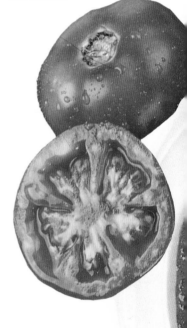

— Steps —

1. Take medium sized, rounded potatoes. Peel
and scoop out the centre then deep fry the shell.
2. Grind mint, coriander leaves, green chillies,
cumin, mango powder, raisins and salt with very
little water into a chutney (relish) and set aside.
3. Heat 90 ml/6 tablespoons oil in a kadhai. Add
turmeric powder, tomatoes, spinach and fenugreek
leaves. Sauté lightly.

4. Add red chilli powder and salt and cook till gravy thickens. Add the yoghurt, garam masala, coriander powder and clarified butter.

5. Remove from heat and push through a thick sieve.

6. Stuff the potatoes with the mint and coriander chutney.

7. Place the potatoes in a shallow dish and pour the hot strained gravy over.

TIPS

Time: Preparation: 45 minutes
Cooking: 1 hour

To serve: Serve immediately with biryani.

POTATO SAAGU

SERVES: 4

A spicy potato delicacy in a thick curry.

— Ingredients —

Potatoes — *600 gms*	Ginger, chopped
Asafoetida (*heeng*)	— *5 gms/1 tsp*
— *a pinch*	Gram (*chana*), roasted
Black peppercorns	— *30 gms/2 tbs*
— *5 gms/1 tsp*	Green chillies — *2*
Cinnamon — *1" stick*	Mustard (*sarson*) seeds
Cloves — *2*	— *5 gms/1 tsp*
Coconut, grated	Onions, chopped
— *30 gms/2 tbs*	— *30 gms/2 tbs*
Cooking oil — *45 ml/3 tbs*	Red chillies, whole — *2*
Coriander leaves, chopped	Salt to taste
— *5 gms/1 tsp*	Tomatoes, chopped
Cumin (*jeera*) seeds	— *30 gms/2 tbs*
— *5 gms/1 tsp*	Turmeric (*haldi*) powder
Curry leaves — *6*	— *5 gms/1 tsp*

— Steps —

1. Wash, peel and dice potatoes in half inch cubes.
2. Make a paste of the green chillies, roasted gram, cumin seeds, black peppercorns, ginger, cinnamon, cloves and grated coconut with a little water in a blender.
3. Heat oil in a kadhai. Add asafoetida, mustard seeds, whole red chillies and curry leaves.
4. When mustard seeds start to splutter add onions and sauté lightly.
5. Add turmeric, stir and add tomatoes. Stir for 2-3 minutes.
6. Add potatoes, salt and sufficient water to cover potatoes. Cover and simmer till tender.
7. Add the prepared paste. Simmer gently for 4-5 minutes.
Note:Saagu can also be made with mixed vegetables.

Time: Preparation: 30 minutes
Cooking: 45 minutes

To serve: Garnish with chopped coriander.
Serve hot with paratha.

TIPS

POTATO & SAGO PATTIE

SERVES: 4

A nourishing teatime snack.

— Ingredients —

Potatoes (boiled) — *5*
Sago — *30 gms/½ cup*
Chaat masala — *5 gms/1 tsp*
Coriander green, fresh
chopped — *15 gms/2 tbs*
Curry leaves — *10*
Ginger — *20 gms/1 tbs*

Green chillies — *3*
Onion — *40 gms/½ cup*
Oil for frying
Red chilli powder
— *2 gms/1 tsp*
Salt to taste

— Steps —

1. Soak sago in 1 cup of water for 1 hour drain and
keep aside.
2. Peel and grate boiled potatoes. Add the deseeded
and chopped green chillies, chopped ginger and
coriander, chopped onions, chopped curry leaves,
drained sago, salt, chat masala and red chilli powder.
Mix well with a wooden spoon in a mixing bowl.
3. Divide into 16 portions and shape into round patties
using a little oil on your palms.
4. Deep fry the patties until they are crisp and golden
brown.

GOBI GULISTAN

SERVES: 4

A crispy carom seeds-cauliflower kebab.

— Ingredients —

Cauliflower, 5 small whole ones, — *1 kg*
Carom seeds (ajwain) — *6 gms/1¹/₃ tsp*
Garam masala — *8 gms/1²/₃ tsp*
Garlic paste — *10 gms/2 tsp*
Ginger paste — *10 gms/2 tsp*
Gram flour (besan)/white flour/maize flour (makke ka atta) — *200 gms/1 cup*
Green chillies, finely chopped — *20 gms/4 tsp*
Green coriander, finely chopped — *20 gms/4 tsp*
Lemon juice — *3 ml/²/₃ tsp*
Oil — *500 ml/2½ cups*
Red or yellow chilli powder — *10 gms/2 tsp*
Salt to taste
Turmeric powder (haldi) — *10 gms/2 tsp*
Yoghurt — *100 gms/½ cup*

— *Steps* —

1. Boil sufficient water to immerse the cauliflowers.
Add salt and turmeric powder.
2. Gradually add the cauliflowers to this brine solution.
Cook for 8-10 minutes over medium heat until the
cauliflowers are half cooked. Drain and keep aside.
3. In a bowl make a batter with the gram flour (besan)/
white flour, carom seeds, lemon juice, yoghurt, ginger,
garlic pastes, garam masala, chilli powder and salt. The
batter consistency should be thick and smooth.
4. Heat the oil in a *kadhai*/wok. Dip each cauliflower
into the batter, coat evenly and deep fry over medium
heat till golden.

TIPS

Time: Preparation: 15 minutes
Cooking: 15 minutes

To serve: Cut each cauliflower in four and
serve on a platter, garnished
with green coriander and
green chillies. Serve with
fresh cucumbers, sliced
tomatoes and mint
chutney.

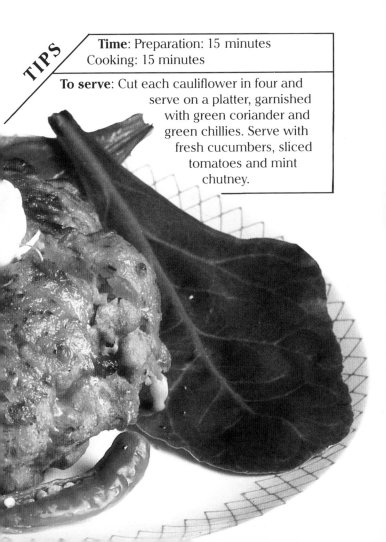

GUNCHA-O-KEEMA

SERVES: 4

This is a rich, crispy, cauliflower preparation.

— Ingredients —

Cauliflower florets — *600 gms*
Butter — *120 gms/½ cup*
Capsicum, diced — *30 gms/2 tbs*
Chaat masala — *2.5 gms/½ tsp*
Chilli powder — *5 gms/1 tsp*
Cooking oil — *15 ml/1 tbs*
Coriander leaves, chopped — *5 gms/1 tsp*
Garam masala — *2.5 gms/½ tsp*
Garlic, chopped — *20 gms/4 tsp*
Ginger juliennes — *5 gms/1 tsp*
Juice of — *1 lemon*
Khoya — *60 gms/4 tbs*
Salt to taste
Tomato purée — *60 ml/4 tbs*
Tomatoes, diced — *30 gms/2 tbs*
Turmeric (*haldi*) powder — *2.5 gms/½ tsp*

— Steps —

1. Heat cooking oil in a kadhai. Sauté garlic. Add cauliflower, turmeric, chilli powder and salt.

2. Cook on low flame till cauliflower is almost tender. Remove and keep aside.

3. In another pan melt butter and toss the capsicum and diced tomatoes in it. Add to the cooked cauliflower.

4. In the same pan brown the khoya till it

14

becomes granulated.

5. Add tomato purée to the cauliflower and cook for a minute.

6. Sprinkle with khoya granules, chaat masala, garam masala and lemon juice.

TIPS

Time: Preparation: 20 minutes
Cooking: 45 minutes

To serve: Garnish with ginger juliennes and coriander leaves. Serve hot with any Indian bread.

KADHAI PANEER

SERVES: 4

Cubes of cottage cheese cooked in a kadhai. A chilli hot, semi-dry and colourful curry!

— Ingredients —

Cottage cheese (paneer) — 600 gms

Black pepper — 8 gms/$1^2/_3$ tsp

Capsicum (green pepper) — 40 gms/$2^2/_3$ tbs

Coriander powder — 10 gms/2 tsp

Coriander seeds — 10 gms/2 tsp

Fenugreek powder (methi) — 5 gms/1 tsp

Garam masala — 8 gms/$1^2/_3$ tsp

Ginger juliennes — 15 gms/3 tsp

Green coriander leaves, chopped
— *15 gms/3 tsp*
Onions, chopped
— *40 gms/¼ cup*
Red chillies, whole
— *15*
Refined oil
— *40 gms/2⅔ tbs*
Salt to taste
Tomato purée
— *150 ml/¾ cup*

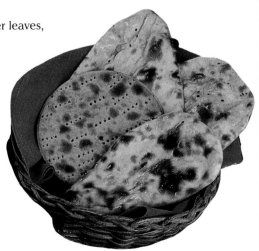

— *Steps* —

1. Cut the paneer into fingers. Cut the capsicum into halves, deseed and make juliennes or cut into small, even squares.

2. Pound the red chillies and coriander seeds with a pestle to a powder.

3. Heat the oil in a *kadhai*/wok and sauté the onions and capsicum over medium heat for 2 minutes.

4. Add the pounded spices and two-thirds of the chopped ginger and stir for 1 minute.

5. Add the tomato purée and salt, bring to a boil and simmer until the oil separates from the gravy.

6. Add the paneer and stir gently for 2-3 minutes.

7. Sprinkle with fenugreek powder, garam masala powder, ground coriander and black pepper. Stir.

TIPS

Time: Preparation: 15 minutes
Cooking: 10 minutes

To serve: Garnish with green coriander leaves and the remaining ginger juliennes. Serve with roti or paratha and salad or raita.

Dum Saunfia Tikka

SERVES: 4

Cubes of cottage cheese, layered with fennel, mint and raisin chutney and grilled in the oven.

— Ingredients —

Cottage cheese — *900 gms*
Carom (*ajwain*) seeds
— *5 gms/1 tsp*
Cream — *60 ml/¹/₄ cup*
Fennel (*saunf*) seeds,
powdered — *10 gms/2 tsp*
Mint chutney
— *120 ml/¹/₂ cup*
Raisins — *30 gms/2 tbs*

Red chilli powder
— *5 gms/1 tsp*
Salt to taste
Sugar — *10 gms/2 tsp*
White pepper powder
— *5 gms/1 tsp*
Yellow chilli powder
— *15 gms/1 tbs*
Yoghurt — *120 ml/¹/₂ cup*

— Steps —

1. Hang yoghurt in a muslin cloth for 2 hours, till whey is drained.

2. Add cream to the yoghurt and mix in red chilli powder, yellow chilli powder, white pepper powder, carom and salt.

3. Add raisins, fennel powder and sugar to the mint chutney.

4. Cut cottage cheese into 1½ inch cubes. Slit the cubes and spread with mint chutney.

5. Press halves together again.

6. Marinade the cheese cubes in the yoghurt-cream-spice mixture for 15 minutes.

7. Put on skewers and cook in a preheated oven at 275 °F for 5 minutes.

TIPS

Time: Preparation: 30 minutes
Cooking: 10 minutes

To serve: Serve hot as a vegetarian cocktail snack.

Paneer Do Piaza

SERVES: 4

Cottage cheese with double the onions.

— Ingredients —

Cottage cheese (paneer), cut into cubes — *900 gms*

Button onions — *300 gms/1½ cups*

Capsicum (green pepper), cut into squares — *150 gms/¾ cup*

Cumin seeds (jeera) — *3 gms/⅔ tsp*

Green cardamoms — *3*

Garam masala — *15 gms/3 tsp*

Green coriander, chopped — *15 gms/3 tsp*

Lemon juice — *10 ml/2 tsp*

Oil — *60 ml/4 tbs*

Red chilli powder — *5 gms/1 tsp*

Salt to taste

Tomatoes, cut into cubes — *150 gms/¾ cup*

Turmeric powder (haldi) — *8 gms/1⅔ tsp*

— Steps —

1. Heat the oil in a pan. Add cardamoms and cumin seed and sauté over medium heat until they begins to crackle. Add the turmeric and red chilli powder and sauté for 30 seconds.

2. Add the capsicum, button onions and tomatoes and sauté for another 30 seconds over high heat.

3. Add the paneer, garam masala and salt and sauté for 30 seconds.

4. Cover and cook for 6 minutes.

TIPS

Time: Preparation: 10 minutes
Cooking: 10 minutes

To serve: Sprinkle with green coriander, lemon juice and serve hot with naan or roti.

PICKLED COTTAGE CHEESE

SERVES: 4

A spicy, pickled dish with cottage cheese.

— Ingredients —

Cottage cheese (paneer), cubed — *1 kg*
Asafoetida (heeng) — *0.5 gms*
Black cumin seed (shah jeera) — *5 gms/1 tsp*
Black pepper, crushed — *6 gms/1¹/₃ tsp*
Cloves — *10*
Fenugreek seeds (methi) — *8 gms/1²/₃ tsp*
Garlic, whole cloves — *6*
Garlic paste — *60 gms/4 tbs*
Ginger paste — *60 gms/4 tbs*
Green cardamoms — *10*
Green coriander, chopped — *10 gms/2 tsp*

Lemon juice — *20 ml/4 tsp*
Mustard seeds (raee) — *7 gms/1¹/₂ tsp*
Olive/mustard oil — *110 ml/¹/₂ cup*
Onions, chopped fine — *200 gms/1 cup*
Red chilli powder — *10 gms/2 tsp*
Red chillies, whole — *16*
Salt to taste
Sugar — *10 gms/2 tsp*
Turmeric powder (haldi) — *10 gms/2 tsp*
Yoghurt, whisked — *300 gms/1¹/₂ cups*

— Steps —

1. Heat the oil in a pan to smoking point. Add the cloves, cardamoms, mustard seeds, fenugreek seeds, whole red chillies and cumin seeds and stir.
2. Add the chopped onions. Reduce the heat immediately and sauté over medium heat until onions are brown.

3. Add the ginger and garlic pastes, red chilli powder, turmeric powder and asafoetida, stir and cook for 3-4 minutes. Add the yoghurt, bring it to a boil and simmer over low heat until the oil separates from the gravy.
4. Add the paneer cubes, salt, pepper, sugar, garlic cloves and lemon juice, stir and cook for 1 minute.

TIPS

Time: Preparation: 15 minutes
Cooking: 15 minutes

To serve: Transfer into a serving dish and garnish with green coriander.

PANEER DAHI KE KEBAB

SERVES: 4

*Crispy sesame seed coated cottage
cheese steak.*

— Ingredients —

Cottage cheese (paneer),
finely grated — *500 gms*
Cardamom powder
— *2 gms/¹/₂ tsp*
Egg white (optional) — *1*
Garam masala
— *10 gms/2 tsp*
Gram flour(besan)/cornflour
— *50 gms/¹/₄ cup*
Green chillies, chopped
— *5 gms/1 tsp*
Green coriander, chopped
— *10 gms/2 tsp*
Mace powder (javitri)
— *2 gms/¹/₂ tsp*
Oil — *100 ml/¹/₂ cup*

Salt to taste
Onions, finely
chopped —
100 gms/¹/₂ cup
Sesame seeds
(optional)
— *100 gms/¹/₂ cup*
White pepper
powder
— *5 gms/1 tsp*
Yellow or red chilli
powder
— *6 gms/1¹/₃ tsp*
Yoghurt, hung
— *400 gms/2 cups*

— Steps —

1. Combine all the ingredients except the gram flour/
cornflour, in a bowl. Mix with wooden spoon and
season to taste.

2. Add the gram flour/cornflour and mix for 2 minutes.

3. Divide the mixture into 20 equal portions. Make each
portion into a round ball, roll it in your
palm and press slightly to get a 4 cm
round patty.

4. Cool the patties in the
refrigerator for 20 minutes.

5. Heat the oil in a deep
pan or a *kadhai*/wok.
Shallow fry in a nonstick
pan until golden crisp.
Alternatively, you could

also lightly coat each patty with egg white.
6. Sprinkle with sesame seeds and shallow fry in a nonstick pan.

TIPS

Time: Preparation: 30 minutes
Cooking: 15 minutes

To serve: Serve with cucumber slices, tomato slices, onion slices and fresh mint chutney.

KALYANI PANEER TIKKA

SERVES: 4

Stuffed, grilled paneer rolls.

— Ingredients —

Cottage cheese (paneer), firm — *500 gms*
For the stuffing:
Black cumin (shah jeera) — *5 gms/1 tsp*
Capsicum (green pepper), chopped — *150 gms/¾ cup*
Cayenne pepper (kashmiri red chilli) — *10 gms/2 tsp*
Coconut powder — *100 gms/½ cup*
Cottage cheese (paneer), grated — *150 gms/¾ cup*
Fenugreek (kastoori methi) — *5 gms/1 tsp*
Lemon juice — *10 ml/2 tsp*
Mushrooms, chopped — *150 gms/¾ cup*
Oil — *75 ml/5 tbs*
Salt to taste

Onions, chopped — *150 gms/¾ cup*
Potatoes, boiled and grated — *100 gms/½ cup*
Raisins — *100 gms/½ cup*
Turmeric powder (haldi) — *5 gms/1 tsp*
White pepper powder — *20 gms/4 tsp*
For the coating:
Cornflour — *100 gms/½ cup*
Cream — *100 ml/½ cup*
Gram flour (besan) — *50 gms/¼ cup*
Green coriander, chopped — *20 gms/4 tsp*
Saffron (a few strands) — *0.5 gms*
Water — *20 ml/4 tsp*

— Steps —

1. Slice the paneer lengthwise into pieces of 15 cm X 6 cm X 0.5 cm.

2. Heat the oil. Add mushrooms, capsicum, onion and coconut powder and sauté.

3. Add the grated paneer, potato and all the spices for the stuffing as well as the lemon juice.

4. Make a thick paste of gram flour and water for coating. Smear the thick paste on one side of each paneer slice, and on the other side put 70-80 gms of the stuffing and make into a roll.

6. Mix the remaining ingredients for the coating.

7. Coat the stuffed paneer rolls with the coating and bake in a slow oven/tandoor for 10-12 minutes.

Time: Preparation: 10 minutes
Cooking: 20 minutes

To serve: Sprinkle the tikkas with chaat masala.
Garnish with grated carrots and lemon wedges.

TIPS

PANEER CAPSICUM DELITE

SERVES: 4

Cottage cheese delicately flavoured with capsicum.

— Ingredients —

Cottage cheese (paneer),
small cubes — *600 gms*
Capsicum (green pepper)
— *150 gms/³⁄₄ cup*
Cumin seeds (jeera)
— *3 gms/²⁄₃ tsp*
Garam masala
— *15 gms/3 tsp*
Green cardamoms — *3*
Salt for seasoning

Green coriander, chopped
— *15 gms/3 tsp*
Lemon juice — *10 ml/2 tsp*
Oil — *60 ml/4 tbs*
Onions — *150 gms/³⁄₄ cup*
Red chilli powder
— *5 gms/1 tsp*
Tomatoes — *150 gms/³⁄₄ cup*
Turmeric powder (haldi)
— *8 gms/1²⁄₃ tsp*

— Steps —

1. Dice the capsicum, tomatoes and onions into small
pieces.
2. Heat the oil in a pan. Add the cardamoms and cumin
seeds and sauté over medium heat until they begin to
crackle.
3. Add the turmeric powder and red chilli powder and
sauté for 30 seconds.
4. Add the capsicum, onions and tomatoes and sauté
for another 30 seconds over high heat.
5. Add cottage cheese pieces, garam masala and salt.
Sauté for 30 seconds, cover and cook for 6 minutes.

TIPS
Time: Preparation: 15 minutes
Cooking: 15 minutes

To serve: Sprinkle with green coriander and
lemon juice before serving.

25

MUSHROOMS WITH PEAS AND SPRING ONIONS

SERVES: 4

*Dhingri Matar Hara Pyaz **is an easy to cook yet delicious mixture of vegetables.***

— Ingredients —

Button mushrooms — 800 gms

Green peas, shelled — 120 gms

Spring onions — 120 gms

Almond paste — 30 gms/2 tbs

Cooking oil — 80 ml/¹/₃ cup

Garam masala
— *5 gms/1 tsp*
Garlic, chopped
— *30 gms/2 tbs*
Onions, sliced
— *120 gms/½ cup*
Red chilli powder
— *2.5 gms/½ tsp*
Salt to taste
Tomato purée
— *240 ml/1 cup*

— *Steps* —

1. Trim, wash and quarter mushrooms.
2. Boil peas till tender, drain and keep aside.
3. Slice spring onions. Chop the green stems of the onions finely for garnishing and keep aside.
4. Heat oil in a saucepan. Sauté chopped garlic till brown.
5. Add sliced onions and sauté till golden brown.
6. Add salt, chilli powder, tomato purée and 240 ml/ 1 cup water and cook for a minute.
7. Remove from fire and strain gravy through a soup strainer into another saucepan.
8. Put back on fire and cook till almost all the liquid has evaporated and the masala is sizzling.
9. Add mushrooms and spring onions and cook for 5 minutes.
10. Add the peas and garam masala and simmer till mushrooms are done.
11. Stir in the almond paste and cook till the gravy reaches a sauce-like consistency.

TIPS

Time: Preparation: 30 minutes
Cooking: 30 minutes

To serve: Garnish with spring onion greens. Serve hot with roti or naan.

CURRIED SPINACH BALLS

SERVES: 4

This curry preparation is also known as Palak Kofta.

— Ingredients —

For gravy
Cashew nut paste
— *30 gms/2 tbs*
Cream — *15 ml/1 tbs*
Coriander leaves, chopped
— *5 gms/1 tbs*
Cumin (*jeera*) seeds
— *2.5 gms/½ tsp*
Garlic paste — *5 gms/1 tsp*
Ginger paste — *5 gms/1 tsp*
Oil — *30 ml/2 tbs*
Onion, chopped
— *1 medium*
Salt to taste
Tomatoes, chopped
— *240 gms/1 cup*
Turmeric (*haldi*) powder
— *2.5 gms/½ tsp*

Red chilli powder
— *5 gms/1 tsp*
For koftas
Spinach — *175 gms*
Gram flour (*besan*)
— *240 gms/1 cup*
Cashew nuts, broken
— *30 gms/2 tbs*
Coriander powder
— *2.5 gms/½ tsp*
Cumin (*jeera*) powder
— *2.5 gms/½ tsp*
Oil for frying
Poppy (*khus khus*) seeds
— *15 gms/1 tbs*
Red chilli powder
— *2.5 gms/½ tsp*
Salt to taste

— Steps —

To make koftas
1. Clean, wash and par boil spinach leaves. Cool, then squeeze out as much water from the spinach as possible and mash.
2. Grind poppy seeds and cashew nuts to a paste.
3. Except oil, mix all remaining ingredients for the koftas with the paste and spinach.
4. Divide mixture into 8 portions. Form balls by rolling each portion between the palms. Heat oil in a kadhai and deep fry the balls. Keep aside.

For gravy
1. Heat 2 tablespoons oil in a kadhai. Splutter cumin

seeds. Add chopped onions and brown.

2. Add ginger and garlic pastes, cashew nut paste, turmeric, red chilli powder and salt and fry for 2-3 minutes.

3. Add chopped tomatoes and fry for another 8-10 minutes. Add 120 ml/½ cup water and simmer.

4. Before serving add the koftas to the gravy and simmer for a few minutes.

TIPS

Time: Preparation: 15 minutes
Cooking: 20 minutes

To serve: Pour into a serving bowl. Garnish with coriander leaves and cream.

HARA KEBAB

SERVES: 4

***Cottage cheese and spinach blended together
to give an unusual green colour.***

— Ingredients —

Cottage cheese, grated
— *450 gms*

Spinach, boiled and blended
— *900 gms*

Cardamom powder
— *10 gms/2 tsp*

Cashewnuts
— *120 gms/½ cup*

Coriander leaves, chopped
— *20 gms/4 tsp*

Garam masala — *20 gms/4 tsp*

Ginger paste
— *45 gms/3 tbs*

Gram flour (*besan*), roasted
— *60 gms/¼ cup*

Green chillies, chopped
— *15*

Mace (*javitri*) powder
— *10 gms/2 tsp*

Oil for deep frying

Salt to taste

— Steps —

1. Mix together all ingredients except oil and shape into
1½ inch round patties.

2. Heat oil in a frying pan and deep fry.

TIPS

Time: Preparation: 30 minutes
Cooking: 15 minutes

To serve: Garnish with onion rings and
serve as a snack or as an accompaniment
with a rice and curry dish.

KADHAI MUSHROOM

SERVES: 4

Mushrooms in a hot tomato curry.

— Ingredients —

Mushrooms — *800 gms*
Black pepper
— *6 gms/1¹/₃ tsp*
Coriander seeds, roasted and crushed — *10 gms/2 tsp*
Dry fenugreek leaves, powdered (*Kasoori methi*)
— *3 gms/²/₃ tsp*
Garam masala
— *15 gms/3* tsp
Garlic paste — *30 gms/6 t*sp

Ginger paste — *30 gms/6 tsp*
Green chillies, slit — *6-8*
Green coriander, chopped
— *15 gms/3 tsp*
Oil — *60 ml/4 tbs*
Onions, chopped
— *100 gms/¹/₂ cup*
Red chillies, whole — *10*
Salt for seasoning
Tomatoes, deseeded and skinned — *350 gms/1³/₄ cups*

— Steps —

1. Trim, wash and cut the mushrooms into halves.
2. Heat the oil in a pan. Add the whole red chillies and chopped onions and sauté for 30 seconds. Add the ginger, garlic pastes and cook over medium heat.
3. Add the garam masala, fenugreek powder and tomatoes and cook over medium heat until the oil separates from the mixture.
4. Add mushrooms carefully and toss over high heat until mushrooms are well coated. Stirring occasionally, cook for 5-6 minutes.
5. Season with salt and sprinkle with crushed coriander seeds and black pepper.

TIPS

Time: Preparation: 10 minutes
Cooking: 15 minutes

To serve: Serve garnished with the green chillies and green coriander.

MASALA DOSA

SERVES: 4

Indian version of stuffed pancakes.

— Ingredients —

For dosa

Parboiled rice — *225 gms*

Lentils (*urad daal*), husked and split — *180 gms/³⁄₄ cup*

Fenugreek (*methi*) seeds — *2.5 gms/¹⁄₂ tsp*

Groundnut oil — *80 ml/¹⁄₃ cup*

Salt to taste

For masala

Potatoes, boiled and mashed — *240 gms/1 cup*

Butter — *30 gms/2 tbs*

Bengal gram (*chana daal*), husked and split — *15 gms/1 tbs*

Cashew nuts, deep fried — *12*

Coriander leaves, chopped — *20 gms/4 tsp*

Curry leaves — *10*

Green chillies, chopped — *4*

Groundnut oil — *60 ml/4 tbs*

Lemon juice — *15 ml/1 tbs*

Mustard (*sarson*) seeds — *5 gms/1 tsp*

Onions, sliced — *120 gms/¹⁄₂ cup*

Salt to taste

Turmeric (*haldi*) powder — *5 gms/1 tsp*

— Steps —

1. To make the batter for dosas, soak the rice and lentils overnight with the fenugreek seeds. Put in a blender with 45 ml/3 tablespoons water and make a fine paste. Remove to a large container and keep aside in a warm place for 3-4 hours; in winter for 5-6 hours.

2. To make the masala, heat oil in a kadhai, crackle mustard seeds in it, add gram and stir until light brown.

3. Stir in onions and sauté until transparent. Stir in green chillies, turmeric and salt.
Add lemon juice.

4. Add potatoes and stir-cook for 5 minutes.

5. Add cashew nuts, curry leaves and coriander.

6. To make the dosas, heat the griddle. Peel an onion and chop into two halves. Tie one half in a muslin cloth, dip in oil and wipe griddle with the flat side to season griddle. This needs to be done only once. Keep griddle on low heat. Spread a ladleful of batter over the entire surface thinly by moving the ladle in concentric circles.

7. Once tiny holes appear on the pancake, sprinkle a teaspoon of oil around the edges and loosen the pancake from the griddle.

8. Slap 2 large tablespoons of the masala filling onto one half of the dosa, drop a knob of butter on it and fold the other half over. Slide off onto a plate.

TIPS

Time: Preparation:Overnight+6½ hours
Cooking: 25 minutes for masala plus
2-3 minutes for each dosa

To serve: Serve immediately with coconut chutney and sambhar.

I D L I

SERVES: 4

A really light and healthy breakfast dish or snack.

— Ingredients —

Lentils (*urad daal*), split and husked — *150 gms/²/₃ cup*

Parboiled rice — *360 gms/1¹/₂ cups*

Oil to grease moulds

Salt to taste

For coconut chutney

Cashew nuts or Gram (*chana*), roasted — *15 gms/1 tbs*

Salt to taste

Coconut, grated — *160 gms/²/₃ cup*

Curry leaves — *8*

Ginger, chopped — *15 gms/1 tbs*

Green chillies, chopped — *5*

Lentils (*urad daal*) — *5 gms/1 tsp*

Mustard (*sarson*) seeds — *5 gms/1 tsp*

Oil — *15 ml/1 tbs*

— Steps —

1. Soak lentils for one hour then put in a blender with very little water to obtain a paste slightly thicker in

consistency than pancake batter.

2. Coarsely grind rice, then wash and soak for 10 minutes.

3. Put the rice flour in a muslin cloth and squeeze out the moisture.

4. Mix the lentil paste with rice flour and salt and set aside for 6 hours to ferment.

5. Grease idli moulds, fill half-way up with batter and steam in a pressure cooker for 8-10 minutes. A needle inserted in an idli should come out clean if the idli is cooked. If no moulds are available then use small, heat proof bowls and steam in a double boiler or egg poacher.

For coconut chutney

1. Grind coconut, green chillies, ginger and cashew nuts/roasted gram to a paste.

2. Heat oil in a kadhai. Add mustard seeds, urad daal and sauté over medium heat. Add curry leaves.

3. Add the ground paste to the tempering. Heat throughly.

TIPS

Time: Preparation: 8 hours 45 minutes
Cooking: 15 minutes

To serve: Demould idlis and place on individual plates. Serve with coconut chutney and sambhar.

Dal Vadas

SERVES: 4

Lentilpatties eaten by itself or served combined with seasoned yoghurt .

— Ingredients —

Gram dal — 300 gms/1½ cups
Coriander (green) — 20 gms/1 tbs
Cumin seeds — 5 gms/1 tsp
Green chillies — 5
Ginger, chopped — 30 gms/2 tbs
Oil for frying
Onions, chopped — 60 gms/½ cups
Salt to taste

— Steps —

1. Soak gram dal for 6 hours.
2. Drain dal and grind coarsely with cumin seeds without much moisture. Remove into a mixing bowl.
3. Add chopped onions, ginger, coriander leaves, green chillies and salt. Mix well with a wooden spoon.
4. Shape into round patties and deep fry in hot oil.
Note: Can be served as a raita, when put in seasoned curds.

TIPS

Time: Preparation: 30 minutes
Cooking: 10 minutes

To serve: Serve with coconut chutney or tomato sauce.

RASAM

SERVES:4

Spicy lentil soup—a traditional South Indian favourite.

— Ingredients —

Toor Dal — *100 gms/½ cup*
Turmeric — *2 gms/1 tsp*
Green chilli — *1*
Tomatoes — *2-3*
Mustard seeds — *4 gms/1 tsp*
Whole red chillies — *5*
Asafoetida — *1 gm*

Garlic (crushed)
— *30 gms/2 tbs*
Curry leaves — *10*
Oil — *15 ml/1 tbs*
Tamarind (pulp)
— *100 gms/½ cup*
Peppercorns — *3 gms/ 3-4*

— Steps —

1. Heat oil in a sauce pan. Add mustard seeds and saute until they begin to crackle. Add whole red chillies, curry leaves, asafoetida and crushed garlic, stir for a few seconds.

2. Add turmeric, washed and cleaned toor dal, quarters of tomatoes, pepper corns, deseeded and slit green chillies, tamarind pulp and salt. Stir and add approximately 1 litre of water.

3. Bring to a boil and let it simmer until dal is mashed.

TIPS

Time: Preparation: 30 minutes
Cooking: 15 minutes

To serve: Serve hot as a starter or an accompaniment to a meal.

SAMBHAR

SERVES: 4

A spicy and sour lentil curry.

— Ingredients —

Green drumsticks, chopped roughly — *200 gms*

Lentils (*toor daal*) — *240 gms/1 cup*

Asafoetida (*heeng*) — *a pinch*

Black lentils (urad daal) — *10 gms/2 tsp*

Coconut paste — *75 gms/5 tbs*

Coconut water — *30 ml/2 tbs*

Coriander leaves, chopped — *20 gms/4 tsp*

Curry leaves — *15*

Coriander seeds — *5 gms/1 tsp*

Cumin (*jeera*) seeds — *10 gms/2 tsp*

Green chillies, slit — *4*

Groundnut oil — *45 ml/3 tbs*

Jaggery — *10 gms/2 tsp*

Mustard (*sarson*) seeds — *5 gms/1 tsp*

Onions, sliced — *180 gms/¾ cup*

Red chilli powder — *5 gms/1 tsp*

Salt to taste
Sesame (*til*) seeds
— *2.5 gms/½ tsp*
Tamarind
(*imlee*) pulp
— *15 gms/3 tsp*
Tomatoes, quartered
— *300 gms/1¼ cups*
Turmeric (*haldi*) powder
— *5 gms/1 tsp*

— Steps —

1. Wash and soak toor daal for 30 minutes.

2. Meanwhile dissolve tamarind in 30 ml/2 tablespoons water.

3. Pound the jaggery and soak in 30 ml/2 tablespoons coconut water.

4. Wash and pat dry black lentils. Wash and pat dry curry leaves.

5. Drain toor daal and put in a handi. Add 1 litre/4¼ cups water, green drumsticks, turmeric, red chillies, green chilli powder, onions, tomatoes and salt. Boil, stirring occasionally till the daal is cooked. Add 1 tablespoon oil and remove from fire.

6. Heat the rest of the oil in a large kadhai, add mustard, sesame, cumin and coriander seeds and the black lentils. Sauté over medium heat till seeds begin to crackle.

7. Add curry leaves, then stir in the asafoetida.

8. Add the cooked daal and tamarind to this tempering. Simmer for 5 minutes.

9. Add the jaggery and bring to a boil.

10. Reduce flame, add coconut paste and simmer for 5 minutes more. Sprinkle chopped coriander and stir.

Note: Can be cooked without green drumsticks too.

TIPS

Time: Preparation: 1 hour
Cooking: 45 minutes

To serve: Serve as an accompaniment to boiled rice, dosa and idli.

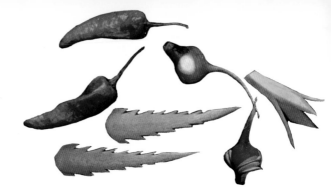

HYDERABADI MIRCHI KA SALAN

SERVES: 4

For the real hot curry eaters, a curry to set you on fire.

— Ingredients —

Green chillies, large — *200 gms/1 cup*
Coconut, desiccated — *50 gms/¼ cup*
Coriander seeds, roasted — *20 gms/4 tsp*
Cumin powder (jeera) — *20 gms/4 tsp*
Garlic paste — *15 gms/3 tsp*
Ginger paste — *15 gms/3 tsp*
Oil — *500 ml/2½ cups*
Onions, sliced — *1 kg*
Peanuts — *50 gms/¼ cup*
Red chilli powder — *12 gms/2½ tsp*

Salt to taste
Sesame seeds (til) — *50 gms/3²/₃ tbs*
Tamarind (imli) — *60 gms/3 lemon sized balls*
Turmeric powder (haldi) — *5 gms/1 tsp*
For tempering:
Cumin seeds (jeera) — *3 gms/²/₃ tsp*
Curry leaves — *20*
Mustard seed — *3 gms/²/₃ tsp*
Onion seed (kalonji) — *3 gms/²/₃ tsp*

— Steps —

1. Soak tamarind in warm water for 10 minutes and squeeze out the pulp.
2. Broil the coconut, peanuts and sesame seeds in a frying pan. Grind to a fine paste.
3. Add the coriander seeds, cumin powder, red chilli powder, turmeric, ginger and garlic pastes and a little salt to this ground pastes and mix thoroughly.

4. Fry the sliced onions in oil till golden brown. Drain from the oil and grind into a paste.

5. Mix the two pastes together.

6. Slit and deseed the green chillies and stuff with the ground paste. Fry the green chillies till they are golden brown.

7. Heat the remaining oil and sauté the mustard seed, onion seed, curry leaves and cumin. Add any left over ground paste and the tamarind pulp and cook on a slow fire for 10 minutes.

TIPS

Time: Preparation: 15 minutes
Cooking: 35 minutes

To serve: Add the fried green chillies and simmer for another 10 minutes and serve.

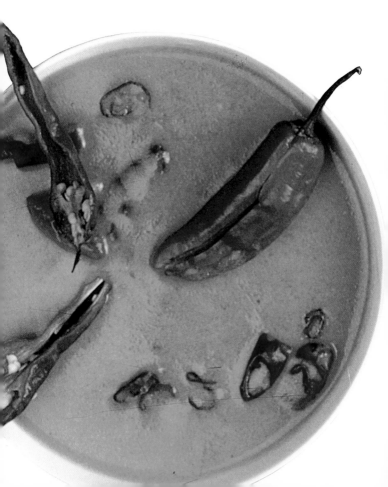

FRIED OKRA

SERVES: 4

*Another coconut flavoured fried okra curry
from the South.*

— Ingredients —

Okra — *800 gms*	Onions, chopped
Cashew nuts — *15 gms/1 tbs*	— *125 gms/½ cup*
Coconut milk — *60 ml/¼ cup*	Red chilli powder
Coriander powder	— *5 gms/1 tsp*
— *15 gms/1 tbs*	Red chillies, whole
Cumin (*jeera*) seeds	— *3*
— *2.5 gms/½ tsp*	Tomatoes, chopped
Curry leaves — *10*	— *240 gms/1 cup*
Grated coconut	Turmeric (*haldi*)
— *80 gms/⅓ cup*	powder — *2.5 gms/½ tsp*
Groundnut oil to deep fry	Lentils (*urad daal*)
Mustard (*sarson*) seeds	husked and split
— *5 gms/1 tsp*	— *20 gms/4 tsp*
Salt to taste	Yoghurt — *120 gms/½ cup*

— Steps —

1. Wash, pat dry and cut the okra into 1 inch pieces.
2. Heat the groundnut oil in a kadhai and deep fry the okra on medium heat till crisp, about 5-6 minutes. Drain and reserve the oil.
3. Put the cashew nuts and the coconut in a blender, add coconut milk and make a fine paste.
4. Heat 75 ml of the reserved oil, add cumin and mustard seeds, urad daal, whole red chillies and the curry leaves. Sauté over medium heat till the seeds begin to crackle.
5. Add onions. Sauté till golden brown.
6. Stir in the tomatoes, then add red chilli powder, turmeric, coriander and salt. Keep stirring till the fat surfaces.
7. Reduce the flame, add the coconut paste and stir again for 2 minutes.

8. Remove from the fire and add yoghurt. Stir, add 400 ml/1²/₃ cups water. Return to heat and bring to boil. Simmer.

9. Add the deep fried okra and cook till gravy seeps in.

TIPS

Time: Preparation: 30 minutes
Cooking: 30 minutes

To serve: Transfer to a shallow dish and serve with boiled rice

CHANA PINDI

SERVES: 4

Chick-pea curry.

— Ingredients —

Chick peas (kabuli chana), whole — *250 gms/1¼ cups*
Baking soda — *5-6 gms/1-1⅓ tsp*
Bay leaf (tej patta) — *1*
Cardamoms, green or black — *3*
Chana masala (aromatic garam masala) — *5 gms/1 tsp*
Cinnamon sticks — *3*
Coriander powder — *5 gms/1 tsp*
Garam masala — *5 gms/1 tsp*
Garlic paste — *10 gms/2 tsp*

Ginger paste — *10 gms/2 tsp*
Lemon juice — *15 ml/1 tbs*
Oil — *60 gms/4 tbs*
Red chilli powder — *4 gms/¾ tsp*
Salt for seasoning
Tea-bag — *1*
For garnish:
Green chillies, whole — *10*
Lemons, cut into wedges — *3*
Onion rings — *100 gms/½ cup*
Tomatoes, medium quartered — *60 gms/4 tbs*

— Steps —

1. Clean, wash and soak the kabuli chana in water for 3 hours.
2. In a heavy pot boil 2 litres of water, add the bay leaf, cinnamon sticks, cardamoms, tea-bag and kabuli chana, and bring back to boil. Add baking soda. Cover and cook over low heat until the kabuli chana is soft. Drain immediately. Remove the bay leaf, tea-bag, cinnamon sticks and cardamoms.
3. Heat the oil in a pan over low heat. Add the ginger and garlic pastes and sauté for 30-40 seconds. Add the red chilli powder, garam masala, coriander powder, chana masala , salt and lemon juice.
4. Add the cooked chanas, mixing carefully.

TIPS

Time: Preparation: 3 hours 15 minutes
Cooking: 1 hour

To serve: Garnish with the onion rings, whole green chillies and tomatoes, with lemon wedges. Serve with Indian breads.

DAL AMRITSARI

SERVES: 4

A staple in all homes across north India, a necessary part of every vegetarian meal.

— Ingredients —

Black beans (urad dal), split and husked — *250 gms/1¼ cups*
Chick peas (chana dal), split — *80 gms/⅓ cup*
Butter — *120 gms/⅔ cup*
Garlic paste — *20 gms/4 tsp*
Ginger paste — *20 gms/4 tsp*
Green chillies — *2*
Mint leaves, chopped — *5 gms/1 tsp*
Oil — *100 ml/½ cup*
Onions, chopped — *50 gms/¼ cup*
Salt to taste
Tomatoes, chopped — *150 gms/¾ cup*

— Steps —

1. Wash the dals in running water and soak for at least 30 minutes. Drain the dals.

2. In a saucepan put 2 litres of water, salt and the dals. Bring to a boil, reduce the heat and simmer. Remove the scum that collects on top of the pan.

3. Add two-thirds of the ginger and garlic pastes, cover and simmer until the dals are cooked and two-thirds of the liquid has evaporated. Mash the dals lightly against the sides of the pan with a wooden spoon.

4. Heat the oil in a pan. Add the onions and sauté over medium heat until light brown. Add the remaining ginger, garlic pastes and sauté until the onions are brown.

5. Add the green chillies, stir for a minute, then add the tomatoes and butter. Cook until tomatoes are mashed.

6. Add the lightly mashed dals to this mixture. Stir for few minutes, until the dal has a medium thick consistency.

TIPS

Time: Preparation: 45 minutes
Cooking: 1 hour

To serve: Garnish with chopped mint leaves. Serve with boiled rice or with a vegetable preparation and rotis.

SPICED SAMBHAR WITH RICE

SERVES: 4

A delicious South Indian dish of hot and sour rice and lentils cooked together. Bisi Bele Huliyana is a complete meal in itself.

— Ingredients —

Basmati rice — *300 gms/1¼ cups*
Lentils (*toor daal*) — *160 gms/⅔ cup*
Asafoetida (*heeng*) — *2.5 gms/½ tsp*
Cardamoms — *5*
Cashew nuts, split — *20 gms/4 tsp*
Cauliflower, small florets — *60 gms/¼ cup*
Bengal gram (*chana daal*), husked and split — *60 gms/¼ cup*
Cinnamon — *2 sticks of 1" each*
Cloves — *5*
Cumin (*jeera*) seeds — *2.5 gms/1 tsp*
Curry leaves — *10*

Fenugreek (*methi*) seeds — *5 gms/1 tsp*
Green peas — *60 gms/¼ cup*
Groundnut oil to deep fry
Groundnut oil for tempering — *30 ml/2 tbs*
Lentils (*urad daal*), husked and split — *30 gms/2 tbs*
Mustard (*sarson*) seeds — *2.5 gms/½ tsp*
Red chilli powder — *2.5 gms/½ tsp*
Red chillies, whole — *2*
Salt to taste
Tamarind (*imlee*) extract — *45 gms/3 tbs*
Tomatoes, chopped — *400 gms/1⅔ cups*
Turmeric (*haldi*) powder — *5 gms/1 tsp*

- Steps —

1. Wash rice and toor daal and soak separately for 30 minutes.

2. To make the masala, broil the gram and urad daal separately on a griddle till light brown.

3. Broil the cinnamon, cardamoms, cloves, cumin seeds and fenugreek seeds separately on the griddle for 30 seconds each. Grind together with the broiled urad daal and gram in a blender.

4. Deep fry the cashew nuts till golden brown. Keep aside.

5. Put toor daal in a handi, add 2.5 litres/10 cups water and bring to a boil. Let simmer until almost cooked.

6. Drain rice and add to the daal with peas and cauliflower and simmer for 10 minutes. Stir occasionally.

7. Stir in the tomatoes, tamarind and the asafoetida.

8. Add red chilli powder, turmeric and salt. Stir in the blended masala.

9. Cover and simmer till lentils and rice are mashed and achieve a porridge like consistency.

10. Sprinkle curry leaves and let simmer.

11. Meanwhile, heat 30 ml/2 tablespoons oil in a kadhai and crackle mustard seeds in it. Add whole red chillies and stir for 15 seconds.

12. Pour the tempering over the lentil-rice mixture. Stir for 2 minutes.

TIPS

Time: Preparation: 40 minutes
Cooking: 40 minutes

To serve: Garnish with cashew nuts and serve with mango pickle and poppadams.

KHUD PUKHT QURESHI

SERVES: 4

Delicacy served in the royal courts.

— Ingredients —

Lentils *(arhar daal)* — *240 gms/1 cup*

Butter or clarified butter *(ghee)* — *120 gms/½ cup*

Cream — *120 gms/½ cup*

Cumin *(jeera)* seeds — *2.5 gms/½ tsp*

Garlic, chopped — *15 gms/1 tbs*

Garlic paste — *15 gms/1 tbs*

Onions, chopped — *120 gms/½ cup*

Pepper to taste

Red chillies, whole — *4*

Salt to taste

Yellow chilli powder — *5 gms/1 tsp*

Yoghurt — *240 gms/1 cup*

— Steps —

1. Pick and wash lentils. Boil with 1 litre/4 cups water, salt and yellow chilli powder till tender.

2. Add garlic paste and cook for a further 10 minutes.

3. Add the cream and yoghurt and 60 gms/¼ cup butter. Cook again for 10 minutes, stirring frequently so that the fat is incorporated into the daal.

4. Heat remaining half of the butter in a pan. Sauté the chopped garlic, cumin and onions for 2 minutes. Add whole red chillies and sauté till brown. Add to the cooked lentils.

TIPS

Time: Preparation: 15 minutes
Cooking: 30 minutes

To serve: Serve hot with a knob of butter and roti.

TAMATAR KA SHORBA

SERVES: 4

A variation of the tomato soup.

— Ingredients —

Tomatoes — *8-10*	Ginger (chopped)
Bay leaf — *2*	— *10 gms/1 tbs*
Butter — *60 gms/4 tsp*	Onions (chopped)
Cardamom — *5*	— *60 gms/½ cups*
Cloves — *6*	Pepper, ground
Coriander fresh, (chopped)	— *3 gms/1 tsp*
— *15 gms/2 tbs*	Refined flour
Garlic (crushed)	— *30 gms/½ cup*
— *10 gms/1 tbs*	Salt to taste

— Steps —

1. Heat butter in a pan, add cloves, cardamom, bayleaf and stir fry till it crackles.

2. Add to it, crushed garlic, ginger, chopped onions are light brown.

3. Sieve in the flour and stir for 1 minute.

4. Add quartered tomatoes and approximately 1 litre of water and let it cook till tomatoes are soft.

5. Pass through a fine sieve into another pan. Season with salt and ground pepper.

TIPS

Time: Preparation: 10 minutes
Cooking: 30 minutes

To serve: Serve hot as an Indian soup garnished with chopped coriander leaves.

Raseele Kum-Kum

SERVES: 4

Tomatoes stuffed with mushrooms.

— Ingredients —

Mushrooms, chopped — *500 gms/2½ cups*
Tomatoes (firm and round) — *15*
Black cumin powder (shah jeera), roasted — *2 gms/½ tsp*
Garam masala — *10 gms/2 tsp*
Garlic, chopped — *15 gms/3 tsp*
Green chillies, finely chopped — *5 gms/1 tsp*
Green coriander, chopped — *10 gms/2 tsp*
Lemon juice — *10 ml/2 tsp*
Mint leaves, chopped — *10 gms/2 tsp*
Oil — *30 ml/2 tbs*

Onions, chopped — *30 gms/2 tbs*
Salt to taste
Tomato pulp, fresh or canned — *100 gms/½ cup*

For the sauce:
Bay leaf (tej patta) — *1*
Cream — *60 ml/4 tbs*
Garlic — *10 gms/2 tsp*
Green cardamoms — *3 gms/²⁄₃ tsp*
Mace powder (javitri) — *3 gms/²⁄₃ tsp*
Oil — *25 ml/5 tsp*
Onions, sliced — *20 gms/4 tsp*
Salt to taste
Tomatoes, chopped — *300 gms/1½ cups*

— Steps —

1. Slice off the tops of the tomatoes and scoop out the pulp. Keep aside the tomato shells and tops.

2. Heat the oil in a pan, sauté the onions, garlic and tomato pulp over medium heat until the moisture is completely evaporated and the oil separates from the gravy.

3. Add the green chillies and chopped mushrooms, stir and cook over high heat for 10-15 minutes till the water evaporates.

4. Add salt, garam masala,

chopped mint leaves, lemon juice, cumin powder and half of the green coriander. Cool the mixture.

5. Fill each tomato with the mushroom mixture and cover with a tomato top. Bake the stuffed tomatoes in a greased baking tray for 15 minutes.

6. For the sauce: Heat oil in a pan. Sauté the bay leaf, cardamoms, onions, garlic and tomatoes. Then add 2 cups of water and salt. Cook for about 30 minutes.

7. Strain through a fine sieve. Transfer the sauce to a saucepan and bring to a slow boil. Add cream and mace powder.

TIPS

Time: Preparation: 15 minutes
Cooking: 1 hour

To serve: Pour the sauce over the baked tomatoes and sprinkle with the remaining half of the green coriander before serving.

Besan ke Gatte

SERVES: 4

A hot Rajasthani speciality which has gramflour dumplings in a gravy.

— Ingredients —

Gram flour — *300 gms/1¼ cups*

Asafoetida (*heeng*) — *a large pinch*

Bay leaves (*tej patta*) — *2*

Cinnamon — *2 sticks of 1" each*

Cloves — *6*

Coriander leaves, chopped — *15 gms/1 tbs*

Coriander powder — *20 gms/4 tsp*

Cumin (*jeera*) seeds — *10 gms/2 tsp*

Garam masala — *2.5 gms/½ tsp*

Ginger, chopped — *15 gms/3 tsp*

Green chillies, chopped — *4*

Mint, chopped — *10 gms/2 tsp*

Oil to deep fry

Oil for gravy — *120 ml/½ cup*

Red chilli powder — *5 gms/1 tsp*

Salt to taste

Soda bi-carb — *a pinch*

Turmeric (*haldi*) powder — *2.5 gms/½ tsp*

Yoghurt — *300 gms/1¼ cup*

— Steps —

1. Mix ginger and half the mint with 60 gms/¼ cup yoghurt and whisk.

2. Add ¼ cup oil, gram flour, 5 gms/1 teaspoon cumin seeds, half the red chilli powder, soda bi-carb and some warm water and knead into a hard, but pliable dough. Divide into 8 and roll into 6 to 8 inch cylinders with the palms.

3. Heat 1.5 litres/6 cups water in a handi. Bring to boil, add the cylinders and boil for 20 minutes.

4. Remove cylinders and set liquid aside. Once the cylinders are cool cut into half inch pieces.

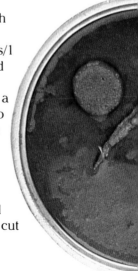

5. Heat oil in a kadhai and deep fry the pieces till golden brown. These are called 'gatte'.

6. Whisk the remaining yoghurt in a bowl, add coriander powder, the left over red chilli powder, turmeric and salt. Set aside for 10 minutes.

7. Meanwhile, heat 45 ml/3 tablespoons oil. Crackle the left over cumin seeds, cloves, cinnamon and bay leaves.

8. Stir in the asafoetida. Reduce flame, add the yoghurt. Stir on low flame till the gravy starts boiling.

9. Add 480 ml/2 cups of the reserved liquid, bring to boil and simmer for 5 minutes.

10. Add the gatte and simmer for 10 minutes. Add remaining mint, green chillies and garam masala.

TIPS

Time: Preparation: 1 hour
Cooking: 30 minutes

To serve: Garnish with chopped coriander leaves. Serve hot with roti.

KARELE MASALE WALE

SERVES: 4

Start with small quantities of the vegetable to acquire the taste. Its blood cleansing qualities make it popular.

— Ingredients —

Bitter gourd — *1 kg*	Salt for rubbing
Black pepper powder	— *45 gms/3 tbs*
— *2.5 gms/½ tsp*	Salt to taste
Dry mango powder	String to
(*amchur*) — *5 gms/1 tsp*	tie the
Oil to shallow fry	gourds
— *120 ml/½ cup*	Turmeric
Onions, chopped	(*haldi*)
— *420 gms/1¾ cups*	powder
Red chilli powder	— *2.5 gms/*
— *2.5 gms/½ tsp*	*½ tsp*

— Steps —

1. Wash, scrape and make long slits on one side of the bitter gourds. Reserve scrapings.

2. Rub 2 tablespoons salt on gourds and mix 1 tablespoon salt with scrapings. Keep in the sun for half an hour.

3. Squeeze the gourds and scrapings between the palms to remove as much moisture as possible. This reduces the bitterness of the gourd.

4. Reserve one fourth of the chopped onions. Mix the rest with the mango powder, black pepper, red chillies and turmeric.

5. Stuff this mixture in the gourds. Wrap the string

firmly round the gourds so that they do not lose their shape while cooking.

6. Heat oil in a pan and shallow fry the gourds, turning over constantly to ensure all sides are done. Remove the gourds.

7. In the remaining oil shallow fry any left over filling, onions, and scrapings.

8. Return gourds to pan. Stir for a minute.

TIPS

Time: Preparation: 1 hour
Cooking: 30 minutes

To serve: Arrange gourds in a flat dish and spread scrapings and onions over them. Serve as an accompaniment with boiled rice and daal

ANOKHI BIRYANI

SERVES: 4

A delightful blend of rice and pulses.

— Ingredients —

Chana dal (split bengal gram) — *25 gms/5 tsp*
Kidney beans (rajma) — *25 gms/5 tsp*
Mung dal (split green beans), washed — *25 gms/5 tsp*
Rice — *150 gms/³/₄ cup*
Toovar dal (pigeon peas) — *25 gms/5 tsp*
Almonds, blanched and fried — *50 gms/¹/₄ cup*
Bay leaves (tej patta) — *2*
Butter — *30 gms/2 tbs*
Cinnamon sticks — *3*
Cloves — *6*
Garlic, chopped — *6 gms/1¹/₃ tsp*
Green cardamoms — *15*
Salt to taste

Green chillies, slit and deseeded — *10 gms*
Mint leaves, chopped — *10 gms/2 tsp*
Onion rings, fried — *20 gms/¹/₄ cup*
Refined oil — *50 ml/3¹/₃ tbs*
Tomatoes, skinned and deseeded — *120 gms/²/₃ cup*
Water — *500 ml/2¹/₂ cups*
Spices to be ground:
Coriander powder — *10 gms/2 tsp*
Cumin powder (jeera) — *5 gms/1 tsp*
Fresh coconut, grated — *150 gms/³/₄ cup*
Red chilli powder — *5 gms/1 tsp*

— Steps —

1. In a food processor grind the coconut, red chilli powder, coriander powder and cumin powder with a quarter cup of water to a fine paste.

2. Clean, wash and soak together the rajma, toovar dal, chana dal for 1 hour.

3. Clean, wash and soak the rice and the mung dal in a separate container for 1 hour.

4. Strain the three pulses. Add 150 ml/³/₄ cup of water and cook over medium heat until tender.

5. Strain the rice, mung dal mixture. Add 1½ cups of water and cook over medium heat until almost cooked. Drain excess water and keep the water aside.

6. Heat oil in a pan. Add cinnamon sticks, cloves, bay leaves, green cardamoms. Sauté for 30 seconds. Add chopped garlic, tomatoes and paste in Step 1. Cook for

4-5 minutes or till the oil separates.

7. Add all the pulses and rice to the pan. Sprinkle a quarter cup of reserved rice. Add salt. Cover and cook on low heat until rice is fully cooked.

TIPS

Time: Preparation: 2 hours
Cooking: 45 minutes

To serve: Remove from heat and garnish with fried onion rings, fried almonds, mint leaves and green chillies and dot with butter.

MORRELS PULAO

SERVES: 4

A delightful blend of rice and morrels.

— *Ingredients* —

Basmati Rice	Onion, chopped
— *500 gms/2½ cups*	— *40 gms/½ cup*
Morrels — *50 gms/1 cup*	Oil — *60 ml/4 tbs*
Bayleaf — *2*	Coriander green, fresh
Cinnamon — *2*	— *20 gms/1 tbs*
Cloves — *1*	Salt to taste

— *Steps* —

1. Wash and soak rice for 1 hour.

2. Soak wash thoroughly the morrels. Slice into thick juliennes and keep aside.

3. Heat oil in a thick bottom pan. Add bayleaf, cinnamon and cloves. Stir till they crackle.

4. Add chopped onions and morrels and stir until onions are transparent.

5. Add drained rice and salt and stir for 1 minute. Add 1 litre of water, bring to boil and simmer till holes appear on the surface.

6. Remove from fire, cover the pan with a tight fitting lid and cook in a pre-heated oven (275 °F) for 7 minutes.

TIPS

Time: Preparation: 15 minutes
Cooking: 25 minutes

To serve: Serve hot garnish with chopped coriander leaves.

TANDOORI SALAD

SERVES: 4

A light, healthy salad, grilled to give it a smooth texture.

— Ingredients —

Capsicum, deseeded and sliced — *150 gms*
Chaat masala — *20 gms/4 tsp*
Cottage cheese, cubed — *160 gms/²/₃ cup*
Garam masala — *20 gms/4 tsp*
Lemon juice — *15 ml/1 tbs*

Lemon wedges — *24*
Onions, sliced — *160 gms/²/₃ cup*
Pineapple slices, drained — *480 gms/2 cups*
Salad oil — *240 ml/1 cup*
Salt to taste
Tomatoes, halved — *300 gms/14-16 pieces*

— Steps —

1. Cut cottage cheese and pineapple slices into 1 inch cubes.

2. Add chaat masala, garam masala, lemon juice, salt and salad oil to the capsicum, onions and tomatoes. Toss well together.

3. Skewer the vegetables, cottage cheese and pineapple cubes in turn.

4. Cook on a slow grill for 10 minutes.

TIPS

Time: Preparation: 30 minutes
Cooking: 15 minutes

To serve: Remove from skewer onto a platter and serve with the lemon wedge.

Mint Relish

SERVES: 4

A fresh, green, tangy relish that is
Pudina ki Chutney **for you.**

— Ingredients —

Mint leaves — *60 gms/¼ cup*
Coriander leaves
— *120 gms/½ cup*
Cumin (*jeera*) seeds
— *5 gms/1 tsp*
Garlic cloves — *2*

Green chilli — *1*
Raw mango, chopped
— *30 gms/2 tbs*
Salt to taste
Tomatoes, chopped
— *45 gms/3 tbs*

— Steps —

1. Clean, wash and chop coriander and mint. Slit and deseed green chillies.
2. Blend all ingredients in a food processor.

Note: As mint discoloures fast, the proportion of coriander must be kept high.

TIPS

Time: Preparation: 20 minutes

To serve: Juice of 1 lemon may be added to make the chutney tart.

Mixed Raita

SERVES: 4

A delicious yoghurt accompaniment to both vegetarian and non-vegetarian meals.

— Ingredients —

Yoghurt — *600 gms/2½ cups*
Black peppercorns — *2.5 gms/½ tsp*
Chilli powder to sprinkle — *a pinch*
Coriander seeds — *5 gms/1 tsp*
Cucumber, chopped — *30 gms/2 tbs*
Salt to taste

Cumin (*jeera*) seeds — *5 gms/1 tsp*
Green chilli, finely chopped — *5 gms/1 tsp*
Mint, chopped — *5 gms/1 tsp*
Onions, chopped — *30 gms/3 tbs*
Tomatoes, chopped — *30 gms/2 tbs*

— Steps —

1. Heat a griddle and broil cumin, coriander seeds and pepper till dark and aromatic.
2. Pound and keep aside.
3. Whisk yoghurt with salt. Add and mix all chopped items.
4. Pour into a glazed earthenware bowl. Sprinkle with chilli powder and the pounded masalas.

Note: 60 gms/4 tablespoons squeezed pineapple chunks can be added for variation.

Time: Preparation: 30 minutes
To serve: Chill before serving.

SPICED YOGHURT

SERVES: 4

Bhuraani Raita **is an easy and quick accompaniment to all biryanies.**

— Ingredients —

Yoghurt — *600 gms/2½ cups*
Cumin (*jeera*) powder
— *2.5 gms/½ tsp*
Salt to taste

Garlic, crushed
—*10 gms/2 tsp*
Yellow chilli powder
— *2.5 gms/½ tsp*

— Steps —

1. Rub crushed garlic with salt.
2. Add to yoghurt and whisk.
3. Reserve a bit of the chilli and cumin powders and mix the rest into the yoghurt.
4. Pour into a serving bowl. Sprinkle the reserved cumin and chilli in a decorative design on the yoghurt.

TIPS

Time: Preparation: 15 minutes

To serve: Chill before serving.

GLOSSARY

Alu: Potato.

Amchoor: Dried mango powder. Lemon juice may be used as a substitute.

Aniseed (Sweet cumin): Aromatic seeds used in meat dishes.

Aromatic garam masala (Chana masala): Ingredients: Green cardamoms 175 gms; cumin seeds 120 gms; black pepper corns 120 gms; cinnamon (2.5 cms) 25 sticks; cloves 15 gms; nutmegs, 2. Makes 440 gms. Method: Grind all the ingredients to a fine powder. Sieve and store in an airtight container.

Asafoetida (Heeng): A pungent resin used in powdered form.

Baigan (Aubergine, Egg plant, Brinjal): Used whole, or in pieces.

Basmati rice: A fine long-grain rice grown mainly in India.

Bay leaf (Tej patta): An aromatic leaf used for flavouring.

Black beans (Urad dal): A black lentil, used whole or split.

Black lentils (Masoor dal): Also known as red split lentils.

Capsicum: Green bell pepper.

Cardamom, green (Chhoti elaichi): A plant of the ginger family whose seeds are used in flavouring.

Cardamom, large black (Badi elaichi): Used in many vegetable and meat dishes, its black pods are used ground whole.

Carom seeds (Ajwain): Also known as thymol or omum seeds.

Cauliflower (Gobi): Used whole or as flowerets to make a dry curry.

Chaat masala: Ingredients: Cumin seeds 65 gms; black pepper corns, black salt (pounded) and common salt 60 gms each; dry mint leaves 30 gms; carom seeds, asafoetida (pounded) 5 gms each; mango powder 150 gms; ginger powder, yellow chilli powder 20 gms each. Makes 445 gms. Method: Grind cumin seeds, pepper-corns, mint leaves and asafoetida together. Transfer to a bowl, mix remaining ingredients. Sieve and store in an airtight container.

Chillies, green (Hari mirch): Fresh chillies used for flavouring and tempering.

Chillies, whole dried red (Sabut mirch): More pungent than green chillies.

Chilli powder (Mirch pisi): Ground dried red chillies.

Cinnamon (Dalchini): An aromatic bark used as a spice.

Clarified butter (Ghee): Made at home but also available commercially.

Cloves (Lavang): Dried flower bud of a tropical plant, used as a spice.

Coconut, grated fresh: Method: Remove the coconut flesh from the hard shell with a knife and grate.

Coconut milk, fresh: Method: Put 2 cups of grated coconut into a food processor. Add 3 cups of water and blend. Sieve and squeeze out all the liquid. Use liquid. Excellent quality tinned coconut milk is available.

Coconut, creamed: Creamed coconut is easily available and can be converted into coconut milk by adding $^2/_3$ cup hot water to $^1/_3$ cup of creamed coconut.

Coriander, fresh green (Chinese parsley or Hara dhania): A herb used for seasoning and garnishing.

Coriander seeds, whole/ground (Dhania): Seeds of the coriander plant.

Cottage cheese (Paneer): Method: Boil 3 litres of milk. Add the juice of one lemon and stir till the mixture curdles. Remove from the fire. Cover and keep aside for 10 minutes. Strain the mixture through a piece of cheese cloth. Tie the ends of cloth together, squeeze out all the liquid, and place under a heavy weight for a few hours. The cheese (300 gms) is now ready for use.

Cumin seeds (Jeera): Available whole; may be powdered.

Cumin seeds, black (Shah jeera, Kala jeera): A caraway-like seed with a flavour that is more subtle than that of ordinary cumin; to be used sparingly.

Curry leaves, fresh and dried (Kari patta): Highly aromatic leaves. Use fresh.

Dals: Dried lentils. The word is used loosely for all pulses.

Dried milk (Khoya): A milk preparation made by evaporating creamy fresh milk. Use milk powder instead.

Dum cooking: This technique is used to improve the flavour of a dish by the method of sealing the lid, generally with dough and cooking on a low flame.

Fennel seeds (Saunf): These seeds are larger but look and taste like aniseeds.

Fenugreek leaves (Methi): A leafy vegetable, considered to be a great delicacy.

Fenugreek leaves, dried (Kasoori methi): Grown only in the Kasoor region of Pakistan, its dried leaves are used in chicken and lamb preparations.

Fenugreek seeds (Methe): Yellow, square and flat seeds with a bitter flavour.

Garam masala: Ingredients: Cumin seeds 90 gms; black pepper-corns 70 gms; black cardamom seeds 75 gms; fennel seeds 30 gms; green cardamoms 40 gms; coriander seeds 30 gms; cloves, mace powder, black cumin seeds, 20 gms each; cinnamon (2.5 cms) 20 sticks; bay leaves 15 gms; ginger powder 15 gms; nutmegs 3. Makes 445 gms. Method: Grind all the ingredients except the ginger powder. Transfer to a clean bowl, add ginger powder and mix well. Sieve and store in an airtight container.

Ginger (Adrak): A root with a pungent flavour. Peel the skin before use.

Gram flour (Besan): A binding agent, used mainly as a batter.

Mace (Javitri): The outer membrane of nutmeg, used as a flavouring agent.

Maize flour (Makki ka atta): Flour made from Indian corn.

Melon seeds (Magaz): Peeled melon seeds are used in savoury dishes.

Mint leaves (Pudina): A herb, used fresh or dried.

Mustard oil (Sarson ka tel): An edible oil extracted from mustard seeds.

Mustard seeds, black (Sarson): A pungent seed, widely used in Indian food.

Nigella Indica (Kalonji): Used in Indian breads, vegetables and fish.

Nutmeg (Jaiphal): A spice, used grated or ground for flavouring sweets and curies.

Parsley: Can be a substitute for green coriander leaves.

Pistachios (Pista): A dried fruit, used in sweetmeats and biryanis.

Pomegranate seeds (Anardana): Used in savouries, and to give a sour flavour.

Poppy seeds (Khus khus): Tiny white seeds used for flavouring.

Rose water (Gulab jal): A flavouring made of fresh rose petals.

Saffron (Kesar/Zafran): The stigma of the crocus flower, grown in the Kashmir valley. Known as the king of spices, it is used for its rich yellow colouring and flavour. Dissolve in water or warm milk before use.

Sambar powder: Ingredients: Coriander seeds 150 gms; cumin seeds 100 gms; black pepper corns 40 gms; mustard seeds 40 gms; fenugreek seeds 40 gms; red chilli, whole 40 gms; turmeric powder 25 gms; Bengal gram 80 gms; urad dal 80 gms; oil 50 ml; garlic powder 20 gms; ginger powder 20 gms; Makes 600 gms. Method: Heat the oil. Sauté all the ingredients on very low heat until evenly coloured. Cool and grind to a fine powder.

Sesame seeds (Til): An oil-yielding seed used for sweets and savouries.

Split green beans (Moong ki dal): A type of lentil, used split or whole.

Spinach (Palak): A leafy green vegetable.

Tamarind (Imli): A pod-like, sour fruit, used as a souring agent.

Turmeric (Haldi): A root of the ginger family used for colouring, flavouring and for its antiseptic qualities.

Toovar dal (Pigeon peas): Also known as toor or arhar dal.

Vetivier (Kewda): An extract made from the flowers of the kewda (*pandanus*) plant used extensively as a flavouring.

Yoghurt (Dahi): Made from milk and used extensively in curries and biryani. Drained yoghurt can be obtained by drip-drying the yoghurt in a fine muslin or cheesecloth for 4 to 6 hours.